To: Miss Virginia

Love,
David Haber

Life's Greatest Treasure

LIFE'S GREATEST TREASURE

*Writings About Discovering
and Cherishing Children*

Selected by Bette Bishop

*Illustrated by
Anne Williams Ziegler*

HALLMARK EDITIONS

A complete list of acknowledgments
appears at the end of this book.

Life's Greatest Treasure

Life's Greatest Gift

A baby is a sweet new blossom of humanity, fresh fallen from God's own home to flower on earth.

GERALD MASSEY

Baby's First Day

Wonder of all wonderment!
Momentous moment when small form
First feels life in itself.
When new eyes open wide
On old, old world.
When tiny hands handle air;
Touch tenderness and love.
When ears first wake to sound
And silent lips find voice and food.
Soon newly-wakened baby wearies.
World will keep.
Being born is quite enough
For one short day.
Baby hands rest; baby mouth yawns;
Baby eyes close in sleep.

PATRICIA WHITE

A Newborn Baby

A baby is God's opinion that life should go on. Never will a time come when the most marvelous recent invention is as marvelous as a newborn baby. The finest of our precision watches, the most supercolossal of our supercargo planes, don't compare with a newborn baby in the number and ingenuity of coils and springs, in the flow and change of chemical solutions, in timing devices and interrelated parts that are irreplaceable.

CARL SANDBURG

Whenever A Little Child Is Born

Whenever a little child is born
All night long a soft wind rocks the corn;
One more buttercup wakes to the morn,
  Somewhere, somewhere.

One more rosebud shy will unfold,
One more grass-blade push through the mold,
One more bird-song the air will hold,
  Somewhere, somewhere.

AGNES CARTER MASON

Choice

Beauty of rich coloring,
Shades of every hue,
But the very loveliest
Of all shades is blue.

Blue is the color
Of an April sky,
Blue is the twilight
Going softly by.

Blue is lake water
Lapping the shore,
And delicate bluebirds
That flutter and soar.

In blue flame of color
Asters run wild,
And blue—innocently blue—
Are the eyes of a child.

KATHERINE EDELMAN

Baby's Eyes

In a baby's eyes,
The wonder of creation
Shines; the miracle
Of new life fresh from heaven,
Of a new soul God has blessed.

KATHERINE DAVIS

Happiness

God sends children for another purpose than
merely to keep up the race—to enlarge our
hearts; and to make us unselfish and full of kindly
sympathies and affections; to give our souls higher
aims; to call out all our faculties to extended
enterprise and exertion and to bring round our
firesides bright faces, happy smiles, and loving,
tender hearts.—My soul blesses the great Father,
every day, that He has gladdened the earth with
little children.

MARY HOWITT

Somewhere the Child

Among the thousands of tiny things growing up all over the land, some of them under my very wing—watched and tended, unwatched and untended, loved, unloved, protected from danger, thrust into temptation—among them somewhere is the child who will write the novel that will stir men's hearts to nobler issues and incite them to better deeds.

There is the child who will paint the greatest picture or carve the greatest statue of the age; another who will deliver his country in an hour of peril; another who will give his life for a great principle; and another, born more of the spirit than of the flesh, who will live continually on the heights of moral being, and dying, draw men after him.

It may be that I shall preserve one of these children to the race. It is a peg big enough on which to hang a hope, for every child born into the world is a new incarnate thought of God, an ever fresh and radiant possibility.

KATE DOUGLAS WIGGIN

Infant Joy

"I have no name;
I am but two days old."
What shall I call thee?
"I happy am,
Joy is my name."
Sweet joy befall thee!

Pretty joy!
Sweet joy, but two days old,
Sweet joy I call thee;
Thou dost smile,
I sing the while;
Sweet joy befall thee!

WILLIAM BLAKE

The First Baby

When the first baby laughed for the first time,
the laugh broke into a thousand pieces and they
all went skipping about, and that was the begin-
ning of fairies.

JAMES BARRIE

A Wonderful Creation

What greater happiness can come to a family than the arrival of a baby! Surely it is a sign that God has blessed the marriage. A baby is God's masterpiece—a wonderful creation of His infinite mind. He has said, "Suffer little children, and forbid them not, to come unto me: for of such is the kingdom of heaven. . . ." No baby can ever be far from the throne of God, the Source of all life, of all creation.

NORMAN VINCENT PEALE

A Prayer for New Parents

O Lord, give us the wisdom—
To deal with our children as You would,
To see in each of them Your Holy Image,
To develop in them a Christ-like love of
all men, not only a select few,
To nurture in them a divine desire to
"put in" and not simply "take out,"
To teach them to be "go-givers" rather
than "go-getters."
O God, in training these dear ones whom
Thou hast entrusted to our charge, help us—

To encourage rather than discourage them,
To discipline with kindness not softness,
To guide them intelligently, not blindly,
To coach, not scold; to nudge, not nag.
Dear Lord, above all, help us—
To use common sense in regard to their
future,
To let them go gladly when the time comes,
To let them lead their own lives while
following them with our love,
To pray always that they will be close to
Thee, not only for the few years of this life
but for the endless years of eternity.

JAMES KELLER

"Of all the commentaries on the Scriptures," wrote John Donne, "good examples are the best."

Our children are watching us live, and what we are shouts louder than anything we can say.

When we encircle them with love they will be loving.

When we are thankful for life's blessings they will be thankful.

When we express friendliness they will be friendly.

When we speak words of praise they will praise others.

When we set an example of honesty our children will be honest.

When we practice tolerance they will be tolerant.

When we confront misfortune with a gallant spirit they will learn to live bravely.

When our lives affirm our faith in the enduring values of life they will rise above doubt and skepticism.

We can't stand there pointing our finger to the heights we want our children to scale. We must start climbing, and they will follow!

WILFERD A. PETERSON

Sweet and Low

Sweet and low, sweet and low,
   Wind of the western sea,
Low, low, breathe and blow,
   Wind of the western sea!
Over the rolling waters go,
Come from the dying moon, and blow,
   Blow him again to me;
While my little one,
   while my pretty one, sleeps.

Sleep and rest, sleep and rest,
   Father will come to thee soon;
Rest, rest, on mother's breast,
   Father will come to thee soon;
Father will come to his babe in the nest,
Silver sails all out of the west
   Under the silver moon:
Sleep, my little one,
   sleep, my pretty one, sleep.

ALFRED, LORD TENNYSON

A Child Asleep

How lovely he appears! his little cheeks
In their pure incarnation, vying with
The rose leaves strewn beneath them.
And his lips, too,
How beautifully parted! No; you shall not
Kiss him; at least not now; he will wake soon—
His hour of midday rest is nearly over.

GEORGE GORDON, LORD BYRON

The Moon

I see the moon,
And the moon sees me;
God bless the moon,
And God bless me.
                    Amen.
CELTIC CHILD'S SAYING

Welcome

The room you have in my heart is new,
I've made it especially nice for you!

I've freshened it with a sun-warmed breeze
That I caught napping in southern seas.

I've swept the floor with a scented brush
That grew in the desert's enchanted hush.

I've walked by the lake where the lupins bloom—
With the peace I found I furnished your room.

The walls I adorned with wistful dreams
Of flaming dawns and twilit streams.

I caught the soft notes of a robin's song—
Its melody lingers all the day long.

I sought the glowworm's golden light
And set it to shine in your window at night.

Beside the slow embers of kindled content
Long thoughts will find encouragement.

My arms will welcome you—keep you warm,
My love will shelter you from the storm.

Where Did You Come From, Baby Dear?

Where did you come from, baby dear?
Out of the everywhere into the here.
Where did you get those eyes so blue?
Out of the sky as I came through.
What makes the light in them sparkle and spin?
Some of the starry spikes left in.
What makes your cheek like a warm white rose?
I saw something better than anyone knows.
Whence that three-cornered smile of bliss?
Three angels gave me at once a kiss.
Where did you get those arms and hands?
Love made itself into bonds and bands.
Feet, where did you come, you darling things?
From the same box as the cherubs' wings.
How did they all just come to be you?
God thought about me, and so I grew.
But how did you come to us, you dear?
God thought about you, and so I am here.

GEORGE MACDONALD

Forbid Them Not

Then were there brought unto him little children,
that he should put his hands on them, and pray:
and the disciples rebuked them.

But Jesus said, Suffer little children, and forbid
them not, to come unto me: for of such is the
kingdom of heaven.

MATTHEW 19:13–14

A Baby's Hands

A baby's hands, like rosebuds furled,
 Where yet no leaf expands,
Ope if you touch, though close upcurled, —
 A baby's hands.

Then, even as warriors grip their brands
 When battle's bolt is hurled,
They close, clenched hard like tightening
    bands.

No rosebuds yet by dawn impearled
 Match, even in loveliest lands;
The sweetest flowers in all the world. —
 A baby's hands.

ALGERNON CHARLES SWINBURNE

Holy Innocents

Sleep, little Baby, sleep;
   The holy Angels love thee,
And guard thy bed, and keep
   A blessed watch above thee.
No spirit can come near
   Nor evil beast to harm thee:
Sleep, Sweet, devoid of fear
   Where nothing need alarm thee.

The Love which doth not sleep,
   The eternal Arms surround thee:
The Shepherd of the sheep
   In perfect love hath found thee.
Sleep through the holy night,
   Christ-kept from snare and sorrow,
Until thou wake to light
   And love and warmth tomorrow.

CHRISTINA ROSSETTI

Baby-land

"Which is the way to Baby-land?"
"Anyone can tell;
　　Up one flight,
　　To your right;
Please to ring the bell."

"What can you see in Baby-land?"
"Little folks in white—
　　Downy heads,
　　Cradle-beds,
Faces pure and bright!"

"What do they do in Baby-land?"
"Dream and wake and play,
　　Laugh and crow,
　　Shout and grow;
Jolly times have they!"

"What do they say in Baby-land?"
"Why, the oddest things;
　　Might as well
　　Try to tell
What a birdie sings!"

"Who is the Queen of Baby-land?"
"Mother, kind and sweet;
 And her love,
 Born above,
Guides the little feet."

GEORGE COOPER

A Family Prayer

Lord Jesus, we would thank Thee that Thou hast blessed our home with the gift of young life, for we know that through our children Thou wouldst remind us of God.

We do resolve, by Thy help, to honor Thee in all our relationships—in our home, so that it may be Thy temple; in our hearts, where Thou dost love to dwell; in our place of business, that it may become an adventure in living our faith.

And now Lord, we place every member of our family in Thy care and keeping. Bless them every one. Be with us all throughout this day . . . In Jesus' name. Amen.

PETER MARSHALL

Heart's Child

She is the sunrise, flaming bright,
A petal unfolding to the light.

The scarlet flash of a cardinal's wing,
The rippling music small brooks sing.

She is the freshness of morning dew,
The loveliness of the rainbow's hue.

The heaven-borne song of the nightingale,
The witchery of a fairy tale.

She is beauty's haunting refrain,
The shining silver of slanting rain.

She is a story just begun
Of love and laughter, heartbreak and fun!

EMILY CAREY ALLEMAN

Why God Made Little Girls

God made the world with its towering trees,
Majestic mountains and restless seas,
Then paused and said,
"It needs one more thing—
Someone to laugh and dance and sing
To walk in the woods and gather flowers,
To commune with nature in quiet hours,"
So God created little girls
With laughing eyes and bouncing curls,
With joyful hearts and infectious smiles,
Enchanting ways and feminine wiles,
And when He'd completed the task He'd begun
He was pleased and proud of the job He'd done,
For the world, when seen through a little girl's
   eyes,
Greatly resembles Paradise.

BARBARA BURROW

Monday's Child

Monday's child is fair of face,
Tuesday's child is full of grace,
Wednesday's child is full of woe,
Thursday's child has far to go,
Friday's child is loving and giving,

Saturday's child works hard for its living,
And a child that's born on the Sabbath day
Is fair and wise and good and gay.

ANONYMOUS

Know You What It Is To Be A Child?

Know you what it is to be a child? It is to be
something very different from the man of today.
It is to have a spirit yet streaming from the waters
of baptism, it is to believe in love, to believe in
loveliness, to believe in belief. It is to be so little
that the elves can reach to whisper in your ear. It
is to turn pumpkins into coaches, and mice into
horses, lowness into loftiness and nothing into
everything—for each child has his fairy godmother
in his own soul. It is to live in a nutshell and count
yourself king of the infinite space; it is

To see the world in a grain of sand,
    Heaven in a wild flower,
To hold infinity in the palm of your hand,
    And Eternity in an hour.

FRANCIS THOMPSON

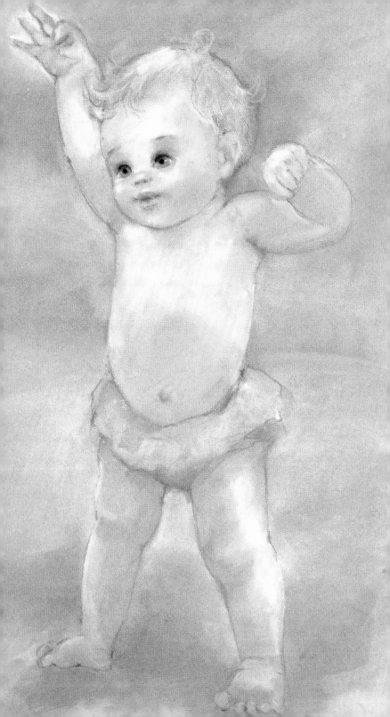

First Footsteps

A little way, more soft and sweet
　　Than fields aflower with May,
A babe's feet, venturing, scarce complete
　　A little way.

Eyes full of dawning day
　　Look up for Mother's eyes to meet,
Too blithe for song to say.

Glad as the golden spring to greet
　　Its first live leaflet's play.
Love, laughing, leads the little feet
　　A little way.

　　　　ALGERNON CHARLES SWINBURNE

Happiness

If there are children around, nothing pleases me so
much as to frolic with them. I find even the
smallest child excellent company, and I am glad to
say that children usually like me. . . . I often tell
them stories or teach them a game, and the winged
hours depart and leave us good and happy.

　　　　HELEN KELLER

To a Granddaughter

My Dear Ellen,

I have received your letter and am very happy to learn you have made such rapid progress in learning. When I left Monticello you could not read and now I find you can not only read but write also. I enclose you two little books as a mark of satisfaction, and if you continue to learn as fast you will become a learned lady and publish books yourself. I hope you will at the same time continue to be a very good girl, never getting angry with your playmates nor the servants, but always trying to be more good humored and more generous tempered than they. If you find that one of them has been better tempered to you than you to them, you must blush, and be very much ashamed, and resolve not to let them excel you again. In this way you will make us all too fond of you, and I shall particularly think of nothing but what I can send you or carry you to show you how much I love you. . . . I have given this letter 20 kisses which it will deliver to you: half to yourself, and the other half you must give to Anne. Adieu my dear Ellen.

THOMAS JEFFERSON

(*written to Eleanor Randolph, November 27, 1801*)

Of Boys and Dogs

The coat of a dog makes a wonderful sponge
For the tears of an unhappy boy.
The neck of a dog is a fine thing to hug
When a small throat is choking with joy.

Courage is greater when faithfully backed
By a tail-wagging amateur sleuth.
Dogs seem to be indispensable rungs
Up the ladder to manhood from youth.

GEORGIA SYKES SULLIVAN

from *The Barefoot Boy*

Blessings on thee, little man,
Barefoot boy, with cheek of tan!
With thy turned-up pantaloons,
And thy merry whistled tunes;
With thy red lip, redder still
Kissed by strawberries on the hill;
With the sunshine on thy face,
Through thy torn brim's jaunty grace;
From my heart I give thee joy, —
I was once a barefoot boy!

JOHN GREENLEAF WHITTIER

Life's Greatest Pleasure

Happy is he that is happy in his children.

THOMAS FULLER

Why God Made Little Boys

God made a world out of His dreams
Of majestic mountains, oceans and streams,
Prairies and plains, and wooded land,
Then paused and thought,

"I need someone to stand
On top of the mountains, to conquer the seas,
Explore the plains, and climb the trees—
Someone to start out small and grow
Sturdy and strong like a tree," and so—
He created boys, full of spirit and fun,
To explore and conquer, to romp and run,
With dirty faces and bandaged shins,
With courageous hearts and boyish grins,
And when He'd completed the task He'd begun,
He surely said "That's a job well done."

PATRICIA WHITE

The Eyes of a Child

A child's eyes, those clear wells of undefiled thought—what on earth can be more beautiful? Full of hope, love and curiosity, they meet your own. In prayer, how earnest; in joy, how sparkling; in sympathy, how tender! The man who never tried the companionship of a little child has carelessly passed by one of the great pleasures of life, as one passes a rare flower without plucking it or knowing its value.

CAROLINE NORTON

To Smile

To smile
Is to see fat puppies
Tumbling in the sun
Or children in a sprinkler,
Kaleidoscope of fun.

To smile
Is to cup a kitten
Gently in your hand,
Or watch small children with buckets,
Engrossed in sea and sand.

To smile
Is to see a duckling
Scamper through spring rain,
Or muse upon the magic
Of childhood joys again.

DORIS CHALMA BROCK

I Believe in Children

I believe in children—little ones, big ones,
chubby and thin ones. There is faith in their
eyes, love in their touch, hope in their
attitude. I thrill with them at life's joys,
run with them through tall grasses, bow
with them in worship, and hold them close
in tragedy. I believe in children—the frag-
ile dream of yesterday, life's radiant real-
ity today, and the vibrant stuff of tomorrow.
Yes, I believe in children, for wherever I
go, to mountain village, industrial center,
or open country, I find yesterday's children
who were nurtured in the things of Christ
at work in the building of the Kingdom of God.

AUTHOR UNKNOWN

Age of Perfection

"One" I thought a lovely age.
  "Two" seemed better still.
"Three!" Ah, that's life's golden stage,
  Rich with many a thrill!
Then, as many a gray-haired man,
  Foolish to the core,
Vowed there's nothing lovelier than
  Little girls of four.

"Four," the time of sparkling eyes,
  Twinkling with delight,
Everything a glad surprise,
  Life exactly right.
Romping all the hours away.
  "Time can have in store
Nothing lovelier," I'd say,
  "Than this age of four."

Now that year has come and gone,
  Never more to be,
Still the charms I look upon
  Glorious are to see.

Still those eyes with gladness glow,
　　Still those charms survive!
All the radiance "four" could show
　　Lovelier seems at five!

EDGAR A. GUEST

Advice to a Young Girl

Lucy, Lucy, my dear child, don't tear your frock:
tearing frocks is not of itself a proof of genius; but
write as your mother writes, act as your mother
acts; be frank, loyal, affectionate, simple, honest;
and then integrity or laceration of frock is of little
import.

And Lucy, dear child, mind your arithmetic. You
know, in the first sum of yours I ever saw, there
was a mistake. You had carried two (as a cab is
licensed to do) and you ought, dear Lucy, to have
carried but one. Is this a trifle? What would life be
without arithmetic, but a scene of horrors . . .? I
now give you my parting advice. Don't marry
anyone who has not a tolerable understanding and
a thousand a year; and God bless you, dear child!

SYDNEY SMITH

July 22, 1835

What Is A Girl?

A girl is a charming and wonderful being
In T-shirt or dress trimmed with lace,
A lover of dolls and little stray kittens—
A creature of beauty and grace.
A girl is a fountain of bubbling laughter,
With pigtails or gay, bouncing curls,
She loses her crayons and pennies and ribbons,
And loves to share secrets with girls.
She likes to play house with some other
                    small "mothers"
Or run down the street jumping rope,
Or climb on your lap for that extra story,
Her heart full of undaunted hope,
She's a lover of tea parties, ice cream and
                    candy,
Of paper dolls, mud pies, and pets,
Of sandpiles and roller skates, makeup and
                    dancing,
And every new doll that she gets,
A girl is a mixture of imp and of angel,
Of wonder and sudden surprise,
With a woman's enchantment and magic and
                    vision,
With stardust and faith in her eyes.

KATHERINE DAVIS

To A Vacationing Child

There are no flowers, I suppose, on the beach, or I would ask you to bring me a bouquet, as you used to at Stratford. But there are little crabs! If you would catch one for me, and teach it to dance the Polka, it would make me quite happy, for I have not had any toys or playthings for a long time. Did you ever try, like a little crab, to run two ways at once? See if you can do it, for it is good fun; never mind tumbling over yourself a little at first. It would be a good plan to hire a little crab, for an hour a day, to teach baby to crawl, if he can't walk, and, if I was his mamma, I *would* too! Bless him! But I must not write on him any more—he is so soft, and I have nothing but steel pens.

And now goodbye, Fanny has made my tea, and I must drink it before it gets too hot. . . . The last fair breeze I blew dozens of kisses for you, but the wind changed, and I am afraid took them all to Miss H____ or somebody that it shouldn't. Give my love to everybody and my compliments to all the rest, and remember, I am, my dear May, your loving friend.

THOMAS HOOD
(*to May Elliot, July 1, 1844*)

What Is A Boy?

A boy is a mischievous, magical creature,
An angel with mud on his face,
A daredevil climber of trees and of rafters,
Who loves any game, any place.
A boy is a keeper of frogs and of beetles,
Whose pockets are stuffed full of string,
An apple, a slingshot, some half-eaten candy
A knife and a new signet ring,
He is found camping out with adventuresome
                    playmates,
Or making a rod and a reel,
Or swinging a bat in an old empty lot,
But can seldom be found for a meal,
He's a bubble gum fan and a comic book reader,
Likes westerns and space ships and noise,
Bicycles, screw drivers, roller skates,
                    bottles,
But most of all likes—other boys.
A boy is a craftsman, a builder, a dreamer,
Whose hopes are as wide as the world,
In the heart of a boy is the hope of the
                    future,
A banner of courage unfurled!

KATHERINE DAVIS

A Father's Prayer

Build me a son, O Lord, who will be strong enough to know when he is weak, and brave enough to face himself when he is afraid; one who will be proud and unbending in honest defeat, and humble and gentle in victory.

Build me a son whose heart will be clear, whose goal will be high; a son who will master himself before he seeks to master other men; one who will learn to laugh, yet never forget how to weep; one who will reach into the future, yet never forget the past. And after all these things are his, add, I pray, enough of a sense of humor, so that he may always be serious, yet never take himself too seriously. Give him humility, so that he may always remember the simplicity of true greatness, the open mind of true wisdom, the meekness of true strength. Then I, his father, will dare to whisper, "I have not lived in vain."

DOUGLAS MAC ARTHUR

To Be A Child

Doomed as absurd adults, we can forget
That stories run through children's heads, the way
Young children run all through a summer day,
Hot in the blazing of the alphabet.
We watch her reading there, wearing her wild,
Utterly-given-up, ravenous look.
But see! It is as if a breathing book
Has picked her up and reads the living child.

This is to be a child: To heighten
Each thing you handle, to be shyer
Than rabbit in wide field, to frighten
Deep dark that scared you, to fly higher
Than kite or hunting hawk, to brighten
Daylight, because you are a fire.

PAUL ENGLE

Life's Greatest Wonder

One of the greatest pleasures of childhood is found
in the mysteries which it hides from the skepticism
of the elders, and works up into small mythologies
of its own.

OLIVER WENDELL HOLMES

Of A Small Daughter
Walking Outdoors

Easy, wind!
Go softly here!
She is small
And very dear.

She is young
And cannot say
Words to chase
The wind away.

She is new
To walking, so,
Wind, be kind
And gently blow

On her ruffled head,
On grass and clover.
Easy wind . . .
She'll tumble over!

FRANCES FROST

Wonder of Life

Children are the most wholesome part of the human race, the sweetest, for they are freshest from the hand of God.

Whimsical, ingenious, mischievous, they fill the world with joy and good humor. We adults live a life of apprehension as to what they will think of us; a life of defense against their terrifying energy; a life of hard work to live up to their great expectations. We put them to bed with a sense of relief—and greet them in the morning with delight and anticipation. We envy them the freshness of adventure and the discovery of life.

In all these ways, children add to the wonder of being alive. In all these ways, they help to keep us young.

HERBERT HOOVER

Of Giants and Castles

Babies do not want to hear about babies; they like to be told of giants and castles, and of somewhat which can stretch and stimulate their little minds.

SAMUEL JOHNSON

Little Raindrops

Oh, where do you come from,
    You little drops of rain,
Pitter, patter, pitter patter,
    Down the window-pane?

They won't let me walk,
    And they won't let me play,
And they won't let me go
    Out of doors at all to-day.

Tell me, little raindrops,
    Is that the way you play,
Pitter-patter, pitter patter,
    All the rainy day?

They say I'm very naughty,
    But I've nothing else to do
But sit here at the window;
    I should like to play with you.

The little raindrops cannot speak,
    But "pitter, patter pat"
Means, "We can play on this side:
    Why can't you play on that?"

ANONYMOUS

47

Foreign Lands

Up into the cherry tree
Who should climb but little me?
I held the trunk with both my hands
And looked abroad on foreign lands.

I saw the next door garden lie,
Adorned with flowers, before my eye,
And many pleasant places more
That I had never seen before.

I saw the dimpling river pass
And be the sky's blue looking-glass;
The dusty roads go up and down
With people tramping in to town.

If I could find a higher tree
Farther and farther I should see,
To where the grown-up river slips
Into the sea among the ships.

To where the roads on either hand
Lead onward into fairy land,
Where all the children dine at five,
And all the playthings come alive.

ROBERT LOUIS STEVENSON

Fancies of Childhood

That season of childhood, when the soul, on the
rainbow bridge of fancy, glides along, dry-shod,
over the walls and ditches of this lower earth.

RICHTER

Color

What is pink? A rose is pink
By a fountain's brink.

What is red? A poppy's red
In its barley bed.

What is blue? The sky is blue
Where the clouds float through.

What is white? A swan is white
Sailing in the light.

What is yellow? Pears are yellow,
Rich and ripe and mellow.

What is green? The grass is green,
With small flowers between.

What is violet? Clouds are violet
In the summer twilight.

What is orange? Why, an orange
Just an orange!

Moon, So Round and Yellow

Moon, so round and yellow,
Looking from on high,
How I love to see you
Shining in the sky.
Oft and oft I wonder,
When I see you there,
How they get to light you,
    Hanging in the air:

Where you go at morning,
When the night is past,
And the sun comes peeping
O'er the hills at last.
Sometime I will watch you
Slyly overhead,
When you think I'm sleeping
Snugly in my bed.

MATTHIAS BARR

Half-Past Three

My friend has a yacht, a house by the sea,
But I have a boy who is half-past three.

I have no jewels, no satin gown,
But I have a boy who is butter-nut brown.

My friend has an orchid, my friend has a rose,
But I have a boy with a freckled nose.

O gull tell the waves that I have no yacht.
Wind, tell the wild forget-me-not

That I have no jewels, no shimmering gown,
No satin slippers, no pillows of down,

But I have a robin, a wind-swept hill,
A pocket of dreams, a heart to fill,

And I have a boy who is half-past three —
A little lad who looks like me.

EMILY CAREY ALLEMAN

Prayer for a Child

When it gets dark the birds and flowers
Shut up their eyes and say goodnight,
And God who loves them counts the hours,
And keeps them safe till it gets light.

Dear Father, count the hours tonight
While I'm asleep and cannot see:
And in the morning may the light
Shine for the birds, the flowers, and me.

    Amen.

     WILLIAM HAWLEY SMITH

Who Has Seen The Wind?

Who has seen the wind?
Neither I nor you:
But when the leaves hang trembling,
The wind is passing through.

Who has seen the wind?
Neither you nor I:
But when the trees bow down their heads,
The wind is passing by.

     CHRISTINA ROSSETTI

Playgrounds

In summer I am very glad
We children are so small,
For we can see a thousand things
That men can't see at all.

They don't know much about the moss
And all the stones they pass:
They never lie and play among
The forests in the grass:

They walk about a long way off;
And, when we're at the sea,
Let father stoop as best he can
He can't find things like me.

But, when the snow is on the ground
And all the puddles freeze,
I wish that I were very tall,
High above the trees.

LAURENCE ALMA-TADEMA

Tell Any Child

Earth,
tell any child who runs you in the spring
   under the froth of buds,
dreams on you under the summer sky or in
   the emerald cave of hemlock,
who scuffs your autumn drifts of roadside
            color,
and flies with flying flakes across your
            breast—
Earth, tell any child
that you are his forever, that he is
the happy owner of a tilting world,
of blossoms by the bushel-basket, tons
of leaves, cloud-shadow-miles, sun, rain
         and snow.
Tell him, Earth,
that he has deed and title
to beauty by the acre
anywhere he breathes!

FRANCES FROST

Dandelions

Dandelions, how did you chance
   to rest upon my lawn?
Are you beds the butterflies forgot to hide
   at dawn?
Are you tiny lanterns dropped last night
   by elves at play?
Are you sparks
   the springtime sun has sent to earth today?
Perhaps you are the brightest locks of gold
   from angel hair—
It seems so strange, for yesterday
   you weren't even there.

MARY LOBERG

Gifts From A Small Boy

His small hands overflowing with rainbow-tinted
   bloom,
He quietly, half-shyly, tip-toed to my room;
"These posies are for you," he said,
Then hurrying through the door,
Left me with more than flowering wreath,
So much—O, so much—more!

KATHERINE EDELMAN

A Child's Laughter

All the bells of heaven may ring,
All the birds of heaven may sing,
All the wells on earth may spring,
All the winds on earth may bring
    All sweet sounds together;
Sweeter far than all things heard,
Hand of harper, tone of bird,
Sound of woods at sundawn stirred,
Welling water's winsome word,
    Wind in warm, wan weather.

One thing yet there is, that none
Hearing ere its chime be done
Knows not well the sweetest one
Heard of man beneath the sun,
    Hoped in heaven hereafter;
Soft and strong and loud and light,
Very sound of very light,
Heart from morning's rosiest height,
When the soul of all delight
    Fills a child's clear laughter.

ALGERNON CHARLES SWINBURNE

Child's Evening Hymn

Now the day is over,
  Night is drawing nigh,
Shadows of the evening
  Steal across the sky.

Jesus give the weary
  Calm and sweet repose,
With thy tenderest blessing
  May our eyelids close.

Grant to little children
  Visions bright of thee,
Guard the sailors tossing
  On the deep blue sea.

Through the long night-watches
  May thy angels spread
Their white wings above me,
  Watching round my bed.

When the morning wakens,
  Then may I arise
Pure and fresh and sinless
  In thy holy eyes.

SABINE BARING GOULD

Acknowledgments

EMILY CAREY ALLEMAN. "Welcome," "Heart's Child,"
"Half-Past Three," copyright 1957 by Emily Carey
Alleman.

PAUL ENGLE. "To Be A Child" from *Poems In Praise,*
© Paul Engle.

FRANCES FROST. "Of A Small Daughter Walking
Outdoors" and "Tell Any Child" by Frances Frost,
reprinted by permission of Miss N. Carr Grace.

EDGAR A. GUEST. "Age of Perfection" from
Living the Years by Edgar A. Guest, copyright
1949; reprinted by permission of Reilly & Lee Co.

JAMES KELLER. "A Prayer for New Parents,"
reprinted by permission of the author.

PETER MARSHALL. "A Family Prayer" from the book
The Prayers of Peter Marshall by Catherine Marshall.
Published by McGraw-Hill Book Company.
Copyright © 1954 by Catherine Marshall. British
publication by Peter Davies Limited.

NORMAN VINCENT PEALE. "A Wonderful Creation,"
reprinted by permission of the author.

WILFERD A. PETERSON. "The Art of Parenthood"
from *The New Book of The Art of Living,* copyright
© 1962, 1963 by Wilferd A. Peterson, reprinted
by arrangement with Simon & Schuster, Inc.

CARL SANDBURG. "A Newborn Baby" from *Remembrance
Rock* by Carl Sandburg, copyright, 1948, by
Harcourt, Brace & World, Inc. and reprinted
with their permission.

Set in Monotype Perpetua, a classic type-face
designed in 1922 by Eric Gill, sculptor and engraver.
Printed on Hallmark Eggshell Book paper.
Designed by Virginia Orchard.